THE
Archive Photographs
SERIES

ABERYSTWYTH

Compiled by
the Aberystwyth Postcard Club

CHALFORD

First published 1996
Copyright © The Aberystwyth Postcard Club, 1996

The Chalford Publishing Company
St Mary's Mill, Chalford,
Stroud, Gloucestershire, GL6 8NX

ISBN 0 7524 0669 8

Typesetting and origination by
The Chalford Publishing Company
Printed in Great Britain by
Redwood Books, Trowbridge

THE
Archive Photographs
SERIES

ABERYSTWYTH

Contents

Foreword

In my capacity as Curator of the Museum of the County of Ceredigion, it always gives me a great thrill to discover old photographs, and in particular, those which I have never seen before. The reader can thus imagine my delight to discover that a complete book of such photographs was to be produced by members of the Aberystwyth Postcard Club.

It is for this reason that it gives me a singular pleasure to write this foreword in support of their publication. The book comprises a collection of some 220 images, primarily taken from original postcard prints, with the vast majority dating from before the outbreak of the Second World War. It provides us with a magnificent record of the Aberystwyth in which our parents and grandparents lived and a fascinating glimpse at the social history of the town. It reminds us of the selfless service given to the town by so many of our forebears, in particular those who contributed to the emergency services – the firemen, the police, the nurses, and of course, our lifeboatmen. It reminds us also of the trials and tribulations which had to be faced by many people in the town – the fires, storms and floods. There were many who gave other forms of service to the community through their activities within the education, transport and retail professions. The book also takes a brief look at many of the characters who lived in the town, and who made all our lives a little more colourful than they might otherwise have been.

The book reflects not only the wide body of knowledge possessed by any society or club having an interest in matters historical, but also much of the research into the history behind their cards which many of the members have undertaken. The information is presented in a light-hearted and informal manner, and this makes the captions a delight to read. These in turn reflect humour and sadness, trauma and tragedy: all elements which surely form a fundamental part of our culture and the fabric of our society and community.

This is a book which has been delightfully presented and well-researched and it reminds us of so many things that we would prefer not to forget. The Aberystwyth Postcard Club are to be congratulated on the valuable contribution they have made to recording the history of the town, through preparing a book which should appeal not only to residents of the town, but also to exiles and visitors alike. It has my wholehearted commendation.

Michael Freeman

Michael Freeman
Curator of the Museum
Ceredigion County Council

The Clarendon Boarding House, Aberystwyth, c. 1910. A group of about twenty-five people prepare to set off on an outing to the countryside. The open sides and solid tyres on the bus must have meant that the trip could well have been quite an exciting ordeal.

Introduction

The collector is often compared to the magpie; he or she hangs on to things in case they may have a value in the future – things which may come in useful some time – and so the 'nest' gets cluttered up with all sorts of bits and pieces. Occasionally, these are 'stashed away' in a box and forgotten for months and, sometimes, even years. Yet, for many of us, the rediscovery of the box, or better still, grand-dad's box, provides a thrill which is very difficult to describe.

The membership of the Aberystwyth Postcard Club is a grouping of such 'magpies' who, once they all get together on the first Monday of each month, share, amidst the 'chatter', the buzz and excitement which is generated by a gathering of people with a common interest, in our case that of 'deltiology' – the collecting of postcards. Collectors, however, find it difficult to remain within boundaries – the Aberystwyth collector will naturally extend his collection to Aberystwyth and district, but then how big is the district? Some have embarked on thematic collecting of, for example, 'pussy cats' or the 'Great Western Railway in Wales'. Many have decided not to confine themselves to postcards, but also to collect old photographs and ephemera. Club members are drawn from all walks of life including a retired Health Service driver who never accepted a penny from those who felt eternally grateful to him for his tender, loving care. When offered old postcards or photographs, however, then the temptation was too great. Every man has his price. We have a retired post-master as one of our members – a mother, daughter, aunt and a grand-daughter who collects 'shiny' cards. We have a retired cleric who is a Fellow of the Royal Philatelic Society, and whose knowledge of all matters related to postal history never ceases to astound us, members drawn from the health and education services, the National Library of Wales, a former personal tutor to HRH The Prince of Wales – such is the composition of the Aberystwyth Postcard Club. New members are always warmly welcomed.

Members of the Club have been collecting postcards for very many years. They scour the postcard fairs, they rummage in antique and 'junk' shops, they know the local 'old folk', many of whose memories extend back to the golden age of Edwardian postcard collecting. It is inevitable therefore that some 'cracking' postcards have found their way into these collections. How I have 'itched' as Club Chairman to have a look at some of these treasures and how I have welcomed the preparation of this book as an opportunity to do just that. Why is it that these old images hold such eternal fascination for us? The answer to this is probably embodied in the word 'change'. The old African mammy-wagons [open-sided buses] often carried the adage that 'No condition is permanent'. Picture postcards have now been commonly used for almost a hundred years and to see those from the first decade of this century reminds us of significant events, important people, changed landscapes, the development of transport, natural disasters and so much more.

The members of the Aberystwyth Postcard Club present in this volume a collection of images drawn from their own personal collections, most, if not all, of which have not previously been published in book form. With Aberystwyth being a 'holiday' town, their joint collections run into many thousands of items. Many meetings of the club have been devoted, therefore, to selecting those images which provide the greatest interest not only to those 'natives' of Aberystwyth, but also to those who visit the town. The commentary reflects the vast body of knowledge jointly possessed by its members. It is sincerely hoped that the images and captions provide as much enjoyment as the preparation of this volume has done. It has been my pleasure and privilege to co-ordinate this effort.

Martin Lewis (Club Chairman)
'Nythfa'
West Street
Newport Pem
SA42 OTD

Baker Street looking east, c. 1900. A group of young people pose for the camera at the turn of the century. The young lady dressed in white is Aberystwyth's oldest resident, Miss Olive Lewis, who is now aged 102 years. At the top right of the picture is situated the statue of Queen Victoria (see page 94).

One

Shops and Streets

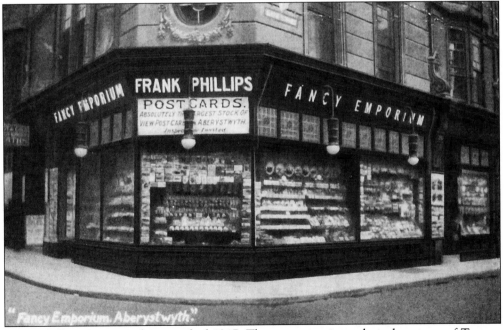

Frank Phillips' Store, card postmarked 1917. The store was situated on the corner of Terrace Road and Bath Street. It was shortly after this time that the Waterloo Hotel, which was situated above the store, caught fire (1919) (see page 30). The quality of the original card is such that the postcards in the window can be identified using a magnifying glass.

Guy's Ironmongery Store, *c.* 1910. This store also occupied a corner position between Bridge Street and Queen Street. The store closed in the late 1950s and the site is now occupied by Carol Ann's Hairdressers.

A. GUY, "Commerce House" Bridge St., & Queen St., Aberystwyth, also 244 & 246, Ladypool Road, Sparkbrook, Birmingham.

MILLINERY,
DRAPERY,
FANCY GOODS,
HABERDASHERY,
STATIONERY,
MATS and RUGS,
GLASS, CHINA,
HARDWARE,
ENAMELWARE,
ALUMINIUM,
BRUSHES OF
ALL KINDS.

Advertising card for Guy's Store. The traders of the town often used the postcard mania of the Edwardian era to promote their own goods and it is interesting to note the range of products which the store had on offer.

Terrace Road, Aberystwyth, *c.* 1914. Rea's Restaurant, which formed part of the White Horse Inn, was taken over in 1864 by one Mr John Rea. Research has revealed that he was the guard on the last mailcoach ever to run on the roads of the United Kingdom.

Great Darkgate Street, Aberystwyth, *c.* 1912. This card shows the main thoroughfare through the town. The town clock standing on the column in the distance provided the town with many years valuable service, and its passing was widely mourned when it was dismantled.

Charley's Dining Emporium, c. 1905. This was located in Portland Road and should not be confused with the store in Cambrian Place bearing the same name. It lays claim to be the first of many fish and chip shops in Aberystwyth.

Phillips the Newsagent's, c. 1910. This store provided the town with sterling service over a period of about sixty years, and was situated on the corner of Chalybeate Street and Cambrian Place. The shop ceased to function as a newsagent's c. 1967 following the death of the last surviving brother. The premises are currently used as a bakery retail outlet.

Crystal Palace Hotel, Queen's Road
c. 1911. It was a Mr Edward Price who
ran this hotel in Aberystwyth for about
thirty years. It was advertised as being no
more than five minutes from the golf
links and two minutes from the sea.

Brynawel Hotel advertising card
published by Ed. Burrow of Cheltenham,
c. 1920. The hotel was situated in Great
Darkgate Street opposite the entrance to
the Castle grounds. Attention was
drawn to the building in June 1935
when its chimney was struck by
lightning.

Jenkins' Newsagents & General Store *c.* 1910. The store was situated at the north end of Northgate. Prior to conversion to a newsagent's, the premises provided the site for the toll-gate which controlled entry into the town from the north. It ceased operation as such in 1869.

Lloyd Family Butchers, Easter 1911. This business was located in North Parade, Aberystwyth, and did a thriving business over many years. As one might expect, the proprietors and the dog look very well-fed.

The Central Fish Shop (seen here *c.* 1910) was situated on the corner of Alexandra Road and Terrace Road. This again should not be confused with a modern fish and chip shop bearing a similar name. This one sold only fresh fish along with poultry and game.

Telegraphic Address: "Randolph Fear, Aberystwyth."
Post Office Telephone: No. 4

TERRACE ROAD, ABERYSTWYTH.

ALSO FRUIT STORES, opposite RAILWAY STATION.

FROM RANDOLPH FEAR,   CENTRAL FISH SHOP.

Dear Sir,

Please let me know your price per ton for old Newspapers & oblige

Yours truly

R Fear.

Advertising card (postmarked 30 May 1916), which was sent to the *Cambrian News*, the writer enquiring as to the cost of old newspapers. This was often used by fish and chip shop owners for wrapping their products, in contrast to the general use today of unprinted paper.

Plâs Crug Lodge and gates c. 1950. The lodge was demolished in the 1950s and gates removed c. 1970. New gates were erected in 1972 a little further back from the main road. These opened onto a pleasant triple avenue leading to the Bowling Green, Cemetery and Council Nursery. Plâs Crug Primary School was built on the nursery site in 1969, the site originally being a turreted mansion.

A winter's scene in North Road, 17 May 1935. Snow scenes in Wales are by no means uncommon, but to have a town centre snow storm in mid-May was an unusual occurrence which clearly made driving conditions very difficult.

Lion Royal Hotel, Great Darkgate Street, c. 1904. This view looks north. The hotel was one of two coaching inns in the town which provided a terminus for coaches plying between Aberystwyth and Shrewsbury.

Great Darkgate Street, looking south, c. 1908. That gas-powered street lamps operated in Aberystwyth at this time, is evident from the card. In fact, this fuel was originally supplied to the town of Aberystwyth in 1834 – an exceptionally early date for public street lighting by this means.

Northgate Street post office situated on the corner with Vaenor Street (card postmarked 1906). With the exception of the main post office in Great Darkgate Street, this was one of six sub-post offices which were established in the town. On the right (and out) of this picture was a small factory which supplied ropes to the ships sailing in and out of Aberystwyth Harbour.

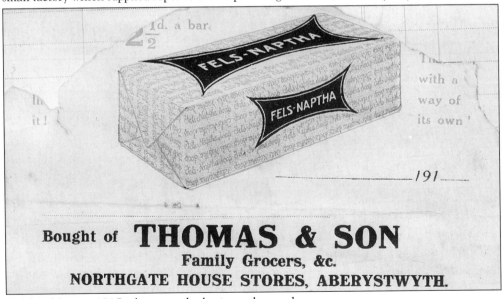

Bill-head from c. 1915 relating to the business shown above.

Portland Street, Aberystwyth, card postmarked August 1927. The Town Hall in the distance was destroyed by fire in 1957 (see page 93). A replacement was built on the same site, and is the building which is used today for most civic functions.

Alexandra Road, card postmarked 1919. All the buildings shown on the left-hand side of the road have been demolished. Those on the right-hand side, however. are relatively unchanged.

North Parade, card postmarked 1906, showing a row of Landau cabs lining the centre of the road. These provided transport for shoppers to all parts of the town, much as taxi cabs do today. The donkey from the beach appears to have lost its way.

North Parade, c. 1950.

Two
Fire and Flood

Over the years, Aberystwyth has had its fair share of natural disasters. This chapter seeks to illustrate how the town has suffered from storm and tempest, fire and flood.

After the storm at Victoria Terrace. Aberystwyth is frequently ravaged by westerly gales and attendant heavy seas. These two photographs show the extent of the damage and devastation caused in 1938.

The storm of 1938 at the height of its ferocity. From the photograph below it can be seen that the foundations of many of the sea-front buildings were threatened by the storm.

Storm damage in Victoria Terrace, 1938. No part of the town was left unaffected by the storms of 1938 and the card shows the extensive damage done to the foundations of some of the buildings in Victoria Terrace.

THE COFFER DAM AFTER THE GALE NOV 23 1938

Repair work commenced immediately after the storms of 1938. The photograph shows a Ruston Bucyrus steam-shovel building a coffer-dam prior to effecting repairs to the foundations of sea-front houses in Victoria Terrace.

Aberystwyth Pier and Pavilion, c. 1910. At one time, Aberystwyth boasted a magnificent pier and pavilion. This was opened originally in 1864. The buildings at the near end of the pier housed equipment for general entertainment, including a cinema. When films of a nautical flavour were shown, the proprietor would open all doors and windows, so that the sea below would enhance odour and sound effects! The cinema remained open during the war despite the danger of mines striking the pillars of the structure.

Aberystwyth Pier and Pavilion, 1938. Those seeking a more leisurely stroll to the end of the pier would find there an aviary used to house all manner of ornamental birds. The storm of 1938 however destroyed the end of the pier, and tragically, the aviary and its inhabitants.

The effect of the floods of 1922 on Smithfield Road (now Park Avenue). Heavy rains and extremely high tides conspired to cause the flood havoc of 1922. The drains became choked with sea-water such that land surface water could not escape.

The floods of 1935. It was recorded in local newspapers that there was a 'disastrous cloudburst on Tuesday evening (28 June), following some exceptionally fine days – two inches of rain fell before midnight. The culvert carrying the brook, which flows from Penglais, became blocked – manhole covers were cast aside allowing water to spout out like a fountain rapidly flooding the hospital'.

The floods of 1935. Walls collapsed allowing the water to flow down Terrace Road, terrorising the residents. For nearly an hour, Terrace Road was an impassable torrent. Basements of houses escaped the ravages of the floods but gardens were badly damaged.

The floods of 1935. Water then flowed into the town, and the residents of Cambrian Square and Llanbadarn Road experienced much damage. Water rushed along Northgate Street into Trinity Road, Poplar Row, Skinner Street and Thespian Street. Barricades built by householders were washed away, paving slabs displaced and a thick layer of mud left behind.

The floods in North Parade, August 1911.

Floods in Llanbadarn Road in 1937, near the junction with Penglais Road. In 1937, there was a cloudburst which caused heavy flash floods on the north part of the town. Water swept down Penglais Hill, forced open the back doors of the houses shown above, and subsequently out through the front doors.

28

Storm damage on Tanybwlch beach in 1938. Tanybwlch beach comprises a very high and substantial wall of stones thrown up by the sea. The above house had been built on a stone foundation, and beyond the ridge of this wall. Occupied for many years by a mother and her daughter, it was, however, not sufficiently substantial to withstand the buffeting of the 1938 storm which caused such devastation throughout the town.

Palladium Cinema fire, 20 February 1935. The cinema stood on the site of the Old Corn Market in Market Street. The Pantyfedwen Trust Building established by Sir David and Lady James of Pontrhydfendigaid now occupies this site.

Waterloo Hotel fire, 1919. This was situated on the sea-front on a site later occupied by the King's Hall. At about 3.00 a.m. on 26 August 1919, a fire broke out at the hotel, and subsequently destroyed the entire structure. The building was so badly damaged by the fire that the remnant shown below was deemed to be unsafe. Many of the residents escaped the blaze by sliding down knotted sheets to the hotel verandah. The photograph shows one of these sheets tied to the verandah.

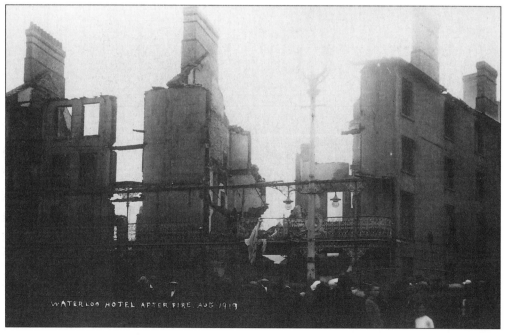

WATERLOO HOTEL AFTER FIRE. AUG. 1919

College Hall fire, 1933. The above wooden-built hall was situated at the junction of North Road with Queen's Avenue. Prior to its destruction, it was widely used for musical concerts and conferences. It is also known to have been used by Lloyd George as a hustings, and by Joseph Parry – the composer of the hymn, *Aberystwyth*.

College Hall fire, 1933. Local photographer Glynne Pickford was taking a stroll one Sunday afternoon, and like all good photographers had his cameral with him. He noticed smoke coming from the direction of the College Hall, and rushed over as quickly as he could. Just as he arrived the roof collapsed, givig rise to the thick smoke seen in the photo.

Storm damage at Plas Crug 1937. A beautiful avenue of elm trees was brought down by high winds in 1937, and few if any were left to remind the public of their former magnificence.

Flood effects on the railway, 1911. The Ystwyth and Rheidol valleys (and railways) have always been susceptible to flooding causing damage to embankments and bridges, and it frequently happened that trains were unable to run. In 1911, the availability of bus transport as an alternative was not so easy as it is today, and passengers such as those shown in the photograph became stranded at Aberystwyth.

Three
The Town's Transport Systems

Donkeys on the Promenade, *c.* 1936. Although donkey rides on the beach and Promenade were popular until relatively recently, it is evident that they were also used to provide donkey-cart rides along the Prom. The starting-point was opposite the King's Hall (formerly the Waterloo Hotel).

Market Hall, St James' Square, *c.* 1925. Public subscription enabled this building to be built in 1824 as a meat market, at a time when the demands of the town required additional trading space. Two markets per week were held here – on Mondays for dairy products (and some meat), and on Saturdays, for meat sales only. At this time, beef and lamb sold for 7d to 8d per pound, mutton for 6d to 7d per pound and pork for a mere 5d or 6d. In 1884, the Corporation took over all stand rental arrangements, and at the same time prohibited the 'pitching' of stands in the street for sales of other food produce.

Pleasure-trips to Devil's Bridge, *c.* 1910. The Llyfnant Valley and Devil's Bridge appeared to be very popular destinations for pleasure-trippers visiting the area. D. & W. Edwards of Hardwick House, Queen's Road set out with a load of passengers in one of their coaches called *The King*, commencing their journey from the Belle Vue Hotel.

Pleasure-trips to Devil's Bridge, *c.* 1910. Another of the coaches owned by D. & W. Edwards was the *General Buller*, and here we see it commence one of its trips from the Promenade (opposite the Belle Vue Hotel).

The Landau cab owners patiently await their fares on North Parade, Aberystwyth (card postmarked 1916). At this time, the street was lined with magnificent trees on each side of the road.

Boarding houses on the sea front, *c.* 1920. By this time, horse-drawn transport had been replaced by the open-sided 'charabanc'. The one displayed is probably providing sight-seeing tours around the town for the residents of the Belle Vue Hotel (situated next door), or possibly a pleasure-trip to Devil's Bridge, the fare for which was three shillings return.

Blodwen, one of the town's horse-drawn omnibuses, which were used to provide transport for tourists visiting Llanbadarn and points further afield.

Aberystwyth's early motor-buses, *c.* 1920. These buses provided public transport to points some 20 miles or more from the town centre. Although the bus has stopped outside the Feathers Hotel at Aberayron (Aberaeron), it advertises a number of businesses at Aberystwyth in particular the Aberystwyth Steam Laundry.

En route to Aberystwyth, *c.* 1920. This bus probably commenced its journey at Aberaeron, but here it has briefly stopped outside the Red Lion Hotel at Llanrhystud (some seven miles from Aberayron). It appears that half the village youngsters have gathered to share the excitement of the event.

Road repair machinery, *c.* 1910. The above machinery was contracted by the Cardiganshire County Council for building and repair of the county's roads. The driver of this particular vehicle was Mr A. Savage. The steam-rollers were used to tow a number of wagons, for example, one to carry tools, one for water storage and another as living accommodation.

Milk delivery float, *c.* 1935. Lluest Farm at Llanbadarn was a 70-acre farm, and was one of a number in the area which processed, bottled and supplied milk to the town. Here we see one of their 'floats' in Park Avenue in Aberystwyth.

Clarach Bay, *c.* 1928. At this time, the beach was one of the few sandy beaches in the area, and consequently very popular with both locals and visitors. Here we see the 'mafia' making one of their regular visits! Clarach is now a site for a large and popular Sunday market.

Private transport in Aberystwyth, *c.* 1920. This magnificent vehicle was owned by the Misses Smith who, at the time, resided at Ffosrhydgaled – now the Conrah Hotel at Chancery. The two lady owners were daughters of Mr Frank Smith – the potato crisp magnate. Their chauffeur was Mr E. Roberts, who later established his own taxi and coach services business.

The New Promenade at Aberystwyth, card postmarked 1938. This is situated just south of the Pier Pavilion and has always been a very popular spot with visitors. The shelters in the centreground were sometimes used for small shows such as the Pierrots, and extensively used for community hymn singing on Sunday evenings.

The Royal Navy visits Aberystwyth, c. 1911. The photograph shows clearly some of the detail of the end of the pier. Large warships have stopped in the bay coinciding with the visit of King George V. Hearsay has it that members of the public were charged 3d to visit the battleships, but 6d to come back!

40

The Pride of the Midlands, c. 1912. One of the vessels which was extensively used as a pleasure-boat was the *Pride of the Midlands*. She was owned by the White Brothers, and George White could often be heard at the extremities of the town shouting 'half-hour trips round the bay'. Regular trips were made to Clarach and Borth, and even as far as Aberdovey when the weather permitted. *The Pride* was finally sold for use as a Thames pleasure-steamer. The voyage around the coast to London took one week, but sailing up the Thames she hit an object near Tower Bridge, sank and was never seen in use again.

Visit of the Sunderland Flying Boat, c. 1950. There were three such aircraft based at Pembroke Dock which were regular visitors to Aberystwyth. When such visits took place, the aircraft would be moored out in the bay, and trips would be organised so that members of the public could inspect and examine the machines.

Alexandra Road and the railway station, *c.* 1930. As can be seen, the road was a veritable hive of activity with buses leaving from outside the station to all parts of the town and the surrounding countryside.

LONDON & NORTH WESTERN RAILWAY

This Company have opened an Enquiry Office at—

69, Terrace Road, ABERYSTWYTH.

until the end of September, 1912, and the Company's representative, Mr ARKINSTALL, will attend daily for the purpose of giving information.

THROUGH CARRIAGES

are run on the following Trains from Aberystwyth and Barmouth.

ABERYSTWYTH to—	BARMOUTH to—
Birmingham (New Street) 1.50 p.m.	
Crewe, 9.5 a.m., 12.10 (until Sept. 16), and 2.30 p.m	Crewe, 11.45 a.m. (until Sept. 16).
Leeds, 9.5 a.m. (until August 31).	
Liverpool, 9.5 a.m., 12.10 (until Sept. 16), and 2 30 p.m.	Liverpool, 11.45 a.m. (until Sept. 16).
London (Euston), 8,10 a.m., 9.5 a.m., and 1.50 p.m.	London (Euston), 8.35 a.m. and 1.30 p.m.
Manchester, 9.5 a.m., 12.10 (until Sept. 16), and 2.30 p.m.	Manchester (London Road), 11.45 a.m. (until Sept. 16).
Shrewsbury 8.10 a.m. and 6.25 p.m.	
Wolverhampton (High Level), 1.50 p.m.	

*Euston Station,
London, July, 1912.*

FRANK REE,
GENERAL MANAGER.

Advertising card of the London & North Western Railway, 1912. The LNWR marketing machine was second to none in the country. It made extensive use of the picture postcard in promoting its services, even to the extent of advocating 'Holyhead as the best route to Killarney' in Ireland! It also used printed cards, such as that shown, for the general dissemination of information to regular clients and other interested parties.

Aberystwyth railway station, *c.* 1939. The original station was built by the Cambrian Railways in the early 1860s. However, at the grouping of all railways into four major companies in 1923, the Cambrian Railway was taken over by the Great Western Railway who later built this imposing façade. From this station, trains ran to Shrewsbury, and to Carmarthen via Tregaron and Lampeter. It was also a terminus for the narrow-gauge Vale of Rheidol line to Devil's Bridge.

Aberystwyth railway novelty card, postmarked July 1914. By lifting the engine's smoke box, a three-inch-wide 'pull-out' shows a total of twelve views of Aberystwyth and the surrounding tourist attractions.

Comic railway postcard, postmarked 1909. With the increasing popularity of Aberystwyth as a holiday destination, there were a number of comic postcard artists who produced cards such as this specifically for the holiday market.

Aberystwyth ticket-collector, c. 1960. A black/chalk board was widely used at the station to advertise railway services. Here, Councillor J. Neville Jones is detailing some services available on the narrow-gauge railway. The board proved useful because train times and other details could be easily and inexpensively altered to meet the changing circumstances.

Aberystwyth railway station, *c.* 1955. A standard-class, 80000 series, tank steam-locomotive awaits its turn of duty with a local train for Machynlleth. The ticket-collector on the station at this time was Councillor Neville J. Jones (see page 44).

Aberystwyth railway station, *c.* 1965. The photograph shows the refurbished station much as it is today. The Carmarthen line on the left has been converted for use by the Vale of Rheidol Railway. A diesel multiple unit was provided for local services at this time, and, on the extreme right, a steam-train prepares to depart for Shrewsbury. The roof-supports are a remnant of the Cambrian Railway architecture. This has recently been restored by Railtrack at substantial cost.

Railmen who helped to run town

WILL O' WHISPERS

WHEN the story of local railways is written down I hope the writer will not forget the contribution railwaymen have made to public life in Aberystwyth.

For 60 years leading railwaymen—engine drivers, footplatemen, clerks and officials—have been prominent in council affairs, trade unions, the Bench and statutory committees of all sorts.

Two of them, Ald. John Joh' and Ald. E. W. Roberts, were both mayor for two separate terms. Another, Cllr. F r e d Foulkes, was mayor in 1943.

The railwaymen formed the first trade union branch in the area way back in 1898. They encouraged other workers to join unions, and in 1912 instigated the setting up of the North Cards. Trades and Labour Council.

Engine-driver Griffith Williams was the first president of the trades council. In 1913 he was the first Labour candidate to stand for the Town Council and was elected top of the poll.

A booking clerk, William Williams, was one of three men who initiated the Co-operative Society movement here. He and guards J. Edwards and E. Shone were on the first committee of the co-op in 1915.

Other leading railwaymen on the co-op committee during the war years and afterwards were David Baker, Charles Williams, J. T. Harget, Dan Davies, George Williams and F r e d Foulkes.

Some of them helped found Cardig...shire Labour Party in 1918 and several stood as Labour candidates for the Council.

Cllr. Dan Davies was one of Cardiganshire's two first Labour Party-nominated J.P.s, appointed in 1929 (the other being Mr. Arnold Smith).

In 1934 local railwaymen helped organise the annual conference at Aberystwyth of the National Union of Railwaymen.

Two of the reception committee were Owen Jones, Mill-street (who retired a few years ago after 50 years on the railway) and D. J. Edwards, Trefechan, who has also retired after lengthy service.

Other committee members were J. Edwards, J. P. James, A. Shone, W. Pugh, D. H. Worthington, H. Shone, L. M. Price, F. Foulkes, T. H. Collins, C. Williams and W. J. Edwards.

In 1943 all three rail unions helped to set up the present Aberystwyth and District Trades Council. R. O. Jones, of the railway clerks, was the first treasurer.

In more recent years Neville Jones was prominent both on the Borough Council and the Trades Council.

The only railwayman councillor to-day is Cllr. Cyril Edwards, though several other railway staff are on other bodies.

★

Here is part five of my year-by-year history of Aberystwyth.

1896—Prince of Wales (later Edward VIII) and Princess Alexandra visit town. Prince is installed as Chancellor of University of Wales, and Princess opens Alexandra Hall. Gladstone awarded honorary degree. Pier Pavilion opened. Ardwyn becomes County Intermediate School (cost £8,500).

1897.—Cliff Railway and Constitution Hill gardens opened. Rheidol Light Railway Act.

1898.—First trade union branch formed in Aber (railwaymen). UCW Central Block opened. Lord Rendel buys Grogythan land for UCW and a national library. Corn, cheese and butter market in Market Street restored.

1899.—Welsh Gazette founded April 27. Bid to ban Sunday newspapers fails in council. Lord Aberdare statue at UCW unveiled. Aberystwyth Baptist College shuts. Salem has first minister. Welsh Industries exhibition here. Llanbadarn Bench refuses drinks licence for Constitution Hill.

1900.—Gasworks near Llanbadarn opened. General election: M. L. Vaughan Davies re-elected. Government inquiry into Aberystwyth proposal of £12,000 extension of promenade around Castle. Italians brought in to work in local lead mines. Volunteer Movement formed here.

The above article appeared in a local newspaper *c*. 1970 and details the service given by the railwaymen to the town.

Four

Hotels and Entertainment

The Queen's Hotel, Victoria Terrace, c. 1934. This was one of Aberystwyth's larger and longer established hotels. It was opened in 1866 and had 104 bedrooms. It also boasted facilities for dancing and conferences. It was commandeered by HM Government during the Second World War for use by the forces and subsequently became County Council offices. The Cardiganshire County Archive is now situated in the base of this building.

The Lion Royal Hotel (card postmarked, April 1906) is one of two original coaching-houses in Aberystwyth from where the Shrewsbury mail-coach left each Tuesday at 4.00 a.m. The building has seen many uses, but the façade remains the same to this day.

The Belle Vue Hotel. In 1863, the hotel was enlarged by the addition of an adjoining house. This enabled the hotel to provide a billiard room and smoking-room facilities. In 1884, it was advertised as having stables and a lock-up coach-house.

'*Hotel Brynawel*'

Tel. 167. ABERYSTWYTH.

R.A.C. — FIRST-CLASS, — C.T.C.

RESIDENTIAL

Boarding Establishment

St. MICHAEL'S PLACE,

Close to Castle Grounds and Parade.

Every Home Comfort. Terms on Application.

Patronised by Colonial Visitors.

Garage Easy Distance.

D. HERBERT.

Hotel Brynawel, St Michael's Place, c. 1910.

The Commercial Hotel, c. 1910. The hotel has now been re-christened the Cambrian Hotel and stands opposite the railway station. As the original name implies, it was favoured by businessmen as well as visitors.

The Talbot Hotel, postmarked 1928. The hotel is centrally situated within the town and is the second of two original coaching-houses in the community. The card shows hotel staff welcoming guests.

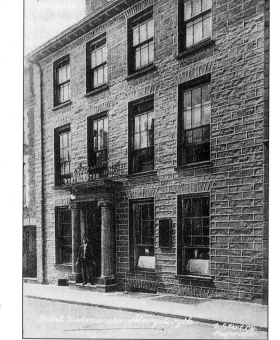

The Westminster Hotel, Bridge Street, c. 1907. At one time this was the home of George Eyre Evans Esq. – the Cardiganshire historian and author of *Aberystwyth and its Court Leet*, published in 1901.

The Coliseum cinema, which was built in 1905 as a variety theatre. The photograph shows Morris John, the projectionist on the left, two unidentified ushers, and also Mr Dick Arfon Jones, the commissionaire. The building now houses the Ceredigion Museum.

Castle Grounds advertising poster, *c.* 1920. Hand-written on the rear of the poster was a draft advertisement: 'Wanted immediately a capable man to drive Hotel and Station Bus. Apply Lion Royal Hotel, Aberystwyth'.

Ellison's Entertainers, 1919. This troupe was one of the foremost groups of entertainers of the time. They were employed annually to provide entertainment at various locations throughout the town.

ABERYSTWYTH CARNIVAL  WEEK

JUNE 19th to 25th, 1932

SUNDAY

United Service in Castle Grounds, 8 p.m.

MONDAY

Opening Ceremony.   Fire Brigade Display

TUESDAY

Arrival of H.M.S's. " Furious " and " Acheron."   Sports 3 p.m.
and 6-30 p.m.

WEDNESDAY

Dog Show, 2 p.m.   Pageant in Castle Grounds, 6-30 p.m.

THURSDAY

Pageant in Castle Grounds, 6-30 p.m.   Naval Sports, 2-30 p.m.

FRIDAY

Launching of Lifeboat. Flitch Trial at College Hall.

SATURDAY

Pigeon Racing 1-30.   Sports 3 p.m. Children— 6-30 ᶠ m

H.M. Ships open for Public Inspection 2 p.m.—6 p.m. on
Wednesday and Thursday.

For full Programme see the Souvenir Guide.

THE PLACE IN THE SUN

Aberystwyth Carnival Week programme, 1932.

Historical pageant in the Castle Grounds, 1934. These were held regularly in the summer season for the entertainment of visitors to the town, and were performed by local residents.

Castle Grounds in 1935. The grounds were often used for musical activities such as sing-songs and community hymn singing. These were particularly popular in the first two weeks of August when, with most industry closed down for its annual vacation, Aberystwyth was a busy resort.

Donkeys on the beach, c. 1920, a major attraction at this time. Their popularity was still high until well after the Second World War and remains so to this day. The portable bandstand is worthy of note.

Aberystwyth Carnival, 1953. The Carnival Queen float usually leads the procession of this annual event. On this occasion, Miss Pat Evans had been elected as Carnival Queen, and her attendants were Misses Doreen Jones, Valmai Edwards, Kay Frances, and Valmai (Borth). The young male assistant was Garrick Dewar.

'The Mayor's official functions', 1935. The Riley Motor Car Company manufactured motor-cars in the United Kingdom since the First World War and, over the years, earned an enviable reputation for design, quality and innovation in the industry. Here we see the Mayor of Aberystwyth, Cllr. David Edwards, extending formal greetings to the Riley Motor Club when it visited the town in May of that year.

Evered Davies and his band, c. 1935. The Davies family had a photographic business in Pier Street for many years, and coupled with this the manufacture and sale of postcards. Within the family, there were a number of talented musicians of whom Evered was one. He formed his own band and was much in demand at local functions and dance halls.

The residents, staff and friends prepare to set out for an outing from the old Bronglais Hospital, Penglais Road, c. 1950. The land on which this hospital was built was once the site for the old Aberystwyth Workhouse (built in 1840 at a cost of £3,000). The old hospital, in the background, was demolished in 1966 to make way for a car park for the new hospital.

The National Sheep Dog Trials, c. 1930. Much like the National Eisteddfod, the venue for the Trials changed each year. About this time, the Trials were held at Aberystwyth on the Vicarage playing fields on Llanbadarn Road.

The portable bandstand, c. 1928. As far as possible, the bands preferred to play at beach level, and for this reason, a facility was provided whereby the bandstand could be lowered down to the beach on rails. During inclement or stormy weather, and during the winter months, the bandstand could once again be drawn back up to Promenade level.

The first permanent bandstand was erected on the Promenade in 1935. It was constructed in an art nouveau-style. The present (permanent) bandstand is an even later version and was built inside the perimeter walls of the 1930s version.

The Aberystwyth Promenade Orchestra posed in front of the original Victorian bandstand in 1938. The photo is known to include its conductor Mr Cheetham along with Ethel Morris (violin), Tal Morris (cornet) and Bill Davies on trombone. Several of the brass players would have been professionally hired from South Wales bands to play during the summer season.

The Aberystwyth Municipal Orchestra, 1941. From left to right, back row, the band comprised: Cecil Hutchings (double bass), David Griffiths (cello), Les Earnest (conductor and violin), Eric Nissen (cello) and -?- (double bass). Front row: Ronnie Hughes, Violet White, -?-, Ronnie Evans, Celia ?, Julie Rogers, D. Rogers, -?-, Billy Buchanan and Haydn Powell. The orchestra played throughout the summer months.

Aberystwyth Town Band, *c.* 1910, with their conductor Mr Jack Edwards of The Bookshop in Great Darkgate Street. The trombonist, second from the left, was Mr Meciah Warrington – grandfather of Don Warrington who plays in today's Town Band.

Aberystwyth Royal Pier Pavilion Band, *c.* 1890, photographed at the end of the Pier. They were one of the original entertainment bands in Aberystwyth.

Uncle Tommy's Minstrels, c. 1939. This was a very popular group in the 1930s which gave two performances daily – in the Castle Grounds, if the weather was fine, and in the Parish Hall if wet. Each morning they proceeded along the Promenade singing aloud in order to draw attention to their shows in the afternoon and evening.

An Aberystwyth rock group, 1963. The young men shown in this photograph were Roy Jones, Chris Edwards, Johnny Humphries, Viv Williams and Peter Lydiard. They formed themselves into a rock group called The Xenons, and resisted many offers to turn professional preferring to pursue their individual careers. This in turn led to the disbanding of the group in 1967. They had an avid local fan club, and are rapturously received whenever they appear at local functions.

The Pierrots, postmarked 1909. The Pierrots were an entertainment troupe who would set themselves up in most seaside towns for the duration of the holiday season. The entertainment scene was deemed to be incomplete without them. They had a very wide repertoire of items, and, at Aberystwyth, they usually performed outside the Castle Walls on the site of the present putting greens.

Things that catch your eye at Aberystwyth

An Aberystwyth novelty card, postmarked 1915.

Five

The Emergency Services

'The Fire Service at Aberystwyth', c. 1928. The original caption to this card may be a misnomer, since the fire brigade in this photograph is simply heading the Carnival Procession along North Parade. The white-fronted building on the right-hand side became Uncle Billy's Amusement Arcade.

Cardiganshire General Hospital, card postmarked July 1910. In 1888, money was given by Mr Joseph Downie, a local bank manager, to build the infirmary on land above North Road. It was the same gentleman's family that had established Downie's Vaults (a public house) in the town in 1810.

Nursing staff at Cardiganshire General Hospital. Differences in headgear are worthy of note. On the extreme left, an 'Army Square' is worn whereas the 'Butterfly' style was tied at the rear. The one worn was a matter of personal choice and did not reflect differences in 'rank' within the system.

St John Ambulance Division, *c.* 1952. The ladies of the force are being inspected on the Promenade by HRH The Duchess of Kent accompanied by Brigadier Evans VC of Lovesgrove. The Belle Vue Royal Hotel can be seen in the background.

Aberystwyth Infirmary & Cardiganshire General Hospital.

OUT-PATIENT'S RECOMMENDATION TICKET

(Subscriber's Ticket),

Available for One Month in 189 5.

I recommend as an Out-Patient ....

aged .... *residing at* ....

being well assured that .... *is a proper object of the charity.*

(Signed) ....

To the Medical Officers of
the Aberystwyth Infirmary.

Out-Patient Hours, from II to I daily, Thursdays and Sundays excepted.
Accidents and urgent cases admitted at all times.

Aberystwyth Infirmary and Cardiganshire General Hospital. The buildings to which this ticket refers have, since this time, been extensively refurbished, and are now used as an extension to Bronglais Hospital with wards providing for the needs of geriatric and mental care patients.

CARDIGANSHIRE EDUCATION COMMITTEE.

Medical Inspection of School Children.

The Committee proposes as an emergency arrangement due to the illness of the School Medical Officer to appoint six Medical men, one for each Union, to complete the Medical Examination of School children by the 31st. December 1917.

Payment will be made at the rate of 2/- per child examined. Particulars as to the number of children to be examined in each Union will be sent on application.

Applications with particulars of qualifications must reach the undersigned on or before Friday 5th. October 1917.

(Signed)   Jenkin James, M.A.,

Director of Education.

24th. September 1917.

A634

Medical inspection of children, September 1917.

A Red Cross nurse, *c.* 1916. Ms D. Bonsall was the daughter of Dr Bonsall – a very well known family in Aberystwyth at this time.

Aberystwyth Ambulance Division, posed against the Old College Buildings in King Street, c. 1940. The division also included the St John Ambulance personnel and totalled about 25 men. Participants were required to pass examinations and administer first-aid as required.

ARP (Air Raid Precautions) staff, posed against the Penparcau Memorial Hall, c. 1940. Many people, both male and female, contributed, in a variety of ways on a voluntary basis, towards the war effort.

Police Barracks, Aberystwyth, *c*. 1911. The Militia Barracks were situated a short distance from the North Gate. The site was purchased from Sir Pryse Pryse and the building erected in 1867 at a cost of £4,000. Sergeants of the staff and regimental bandsmen were quartered here, but the building was not large enough to accommodate the entire regiment.

The Cardiganshire Police Force at Aberystwyth, *c*. 1910.

Cardiganshire Constabulary

This is to Certify

that   Evan Richard DAVIES   joined the

Cardiganshire Constabulary on the 14th May, 1941

and left on the 4th October, 1952.

Period of Service   11   years   144   days
Cause of Leaving   At own request.
Rank on Leaving   Police Constable.
His Conduct in the Police Force was   Satisfactory.
Previous Service in Police or H.M. Forces   None.

Personal Description:

Date of Birth 20th December, 1897 Place of Birth   Llangeitho, Cards.
Height   5 feet 10 inches.   Build   Proportionate.
Complexion   Fresh.   Eyes   Brown.   Hair   Dark.
Distinguishing Marks   Scar under left ear.

Chief Constable's Office
    Aberystwyth

Date   4th October,   19 52.

                                        Chief Constable

Certificate of enlisting in the Cardiganshire Constabulary, 1952. A certificate such as this was given to all those joining the Constabulary; it was awarded to one of the recruits shown on page 70.

The Cardiganshire Police Force, 1941. The old Police Station, Great Darkgate Street, was built in 1888 on the site of the 'house of correction', which in turn had been erected at the Great Dark Gate in the thirteenth century. The old Police Station was demolished in 1975.

The Mayor's Sunday, North Parade, c. 1957. This event forms part of the social calendar of the town. The procession has representatives from a substantial number of the 'professions' in Aberystwyth. The police section here is led by Superintendent R.E. Davies and Inspector Havard.

Aberystwyth Fire Service, *c.* 1925. The full fire-fighting service of the town is posed in a field at Aberystwyth. In addition to the main fire-engine, the force had two motor-cars and three trailered fire-tenders.

Auxiliary Fire Station staff at Aberystwyth. These were part-time members of staff who were frequently called upon to support the efforts of their full-time colleagues. The group is known to include Glyn Pickford (photographer), Danny Lewis ('Danny the Sweets'), Lloyd (the insurance), Phillips (the coal), Richards (the fruiterer) and Moc Rees ('Moc Bach') of the *Cambrian News.*

Full-time Fire Station staff posed against the walls of the National Library of Wales, c. 1925. The Leyland fire-engine has solid tyres, and even though there were fire-hydrants situated strategically throughout the town, the engines also carried a considerable amount of their own water.

The Aberystwyth lifeboat, c. 1895. The boat and crew are posed against the lifeboat house in Queen's Road. The building ceased to be used for this purpose c. 1965. It has recently been acquired by the BBC and is used as their local broadcasting studio.

Aberystwyth lifeboat, card postmarked 1906. At this time the lifeboat was kept in the lifeboat house in Queen's Road, some distance from the sea. When signals were fired, a team of four horses was used to draw the lifeboat along the Promenade to its launching-point. At this time the lifeboat was powered by 'oars', or by sail if wind directions proved favourable.

Aberystwyth lifeboat, c. 1906. While horses would bring the lifeboat to the launch-ramp, a team of men was used to control the roll of the carriage and lifeboat into the water. At about this time, plans to purchase premises opposite the launch-ramp, for use as a lifeboat house ultimately came to nothing.

'The Return of the Lifeboat', *c.* 1955. As lifeboats became more modern, and heavier, they could no longer be handled by man-power. A tracked vehicle was necessary to work on the shingle beach, and this was used to haul the lifeboat back onto its carriage, and thence to the lifeboat house.

The Royal National Lifeboat Institution (RNLI), *c.* 1950, showing a number of men, all of whom, at one time or another, acted as coxswain of the Aberystwyth lifeboat. On the left is John Nicoll who was the last coxswain of the lifeboat. Others, from left to right are: Danny 'Colenso' Davies, Baden Davies, Evan Daniel, Jackie Jenkins and Ben White.

Six

Education and Youth Activities

This comic card (from c. 1907) by local artist Howard Lloyd Roberts reflects the fact that Aberystwyth is a town which has always placed a great emphasis on education. In recent years, it has boasted a university, national colleges of librarianship and agriculture, a college of further education, two secondary schools and numerous primary schools.

National School, Aberystwyth, *c*. 1908. Situated in North Road, the school was built in 1866 with accommodation for 600 pupils. Her Majesty's Inspectors reported in 1879 that 'this school's teaching is of a satisfactory order, and has made fair progress in the past year'. In 1951, it was made into an English-speaking primary school. It was demolished in 1988 to make room for thirty-two privately-owned flats.

Ardwyn School Dramatic Society, card postmarked 1905. The message on the rear of the postcard reads: 'I am sending you a postcard of a Chinese play which came off grand – they are thinking of having it over again…'.

Aberystwyth Board School, Alexandra Road. By advertising in the *Western Mail*, the *Aberystwyth Observer*, *Cambrian News* and other newspapers, tenders were invited in 1872 for building the school. Two were received, and that of Thomas Davies for the sum of £3,395 was accepted. The headmaster's salary at this time was £12.10s per annum.

Board School admission ticket, 1872.

CARDIGANSHIRE EDUCATION COMMITTEE

The following posts are now vacant :-

ALEXANDRA RD. COUNCIL SCHOOL, ABERYSTWYTH (Girls Department).
Headteacher, Salary £120, rising to £150 per annum by biennial
increments of £5. Knowledge of Welsh desirable and previous
experience extending over some years essential. Number of
girls on registers 240. The School is a Practising School in
connection with the Day Training Department, University College
of Wales, Aberystwyth, and the late Headteacher acted as Instructress
in Needlework on the staff of the Day Training Department, for which
work she received £30 per annum.

SILIAN C OF E SCHOOL (Nr. Lampeter). Female Certificate Headteacher.
Salary £70 per annum.

ALEXANDRA RD. COUNCIL SCHOOL, ABERYSTWYTH (Infants Department.)
Female Uncertificated Teacher. Salary £30 - £40 according to
experience.

CERTIFICATED Assistant Teachers are required at the undermentioned Schools +-
Salary £70 per annum :-

New Quay C.   Llangeitho C.
Pontrhydfendigaid C.

Applications on forms to be obtained from the undersigned on receipt
of a stamped addressed envelope should be accompanied by copies of
three recent testimonials, and should reach me on or before WEDNESDAY
15th February, 1911.

JENKIN JAMES, M.A.
Director of Education,
A v e r y s t w y t h.

31st January, 1911.

R974

Draft advertisement by Cardiganshire Education Committee, 1911. The salaries payable are
worthy of note.

The YWCA Brownie Pack participate in the Mayor's Sunday Parade, *c.* 1960. Here they march along Queen's Road in the charge of Brown Owl Doreen Davies and Tawny Owl Anne Parry.

Aberystwyth Boy Scouts, *c.* 1910, pictured making one of their excursions to Tanybwlch beach to the south of Aberystwyth. It is interesting to note that they are wearing the original Boy Scout uniforms designed by Baden Powell.

Rheidol Juvenile Choir, 1911. This photograph was taken outside the Siloh Chapel schoolroom in Queen's Road; the chapel was built in 1863. It is possible that most of the choristers were drawn from the Sunday school membership of this chapel.

Cast of the English Primary School Nativity play, c. 1968.

NERTH Dysg ei YMDRECH
20/6/03

Should auld acquaintance be forgot?
Ne never brought to min'
Should old acquaintance be forgot
And days of auld lang syne.
The Sixth
The Sixth
Our noble Sixth.

Ardwyn County School (view postmarked July 1903), became the secondary school for Aberystwyth. When it was completed in 1896 it was originally intended for sixty-five boys. However, in 1898, the school was opened for girls as well. Sixty years later, the population of Aberystwyth had grown such that the Dinas secondary modern school was established (at Waunfawr) *c.* 1960 – a school which has now become the Penglais Comprehensive School.

Prefects at Ardwyn, academic year 1932-33. From left to right, front row: Dorothy Baird, Margaret Morgan, Mary de Lloyd, Annie Davies, Mary Richard, Megan Jones and Arduful Jones. Middle row: Daphne Loveday, David Sainsbury, Glanville Griffiths, Ivor Snell, John James, Stanley Cheetham and Nancy Jenkins. Back row: Ronald Richards, Noel Butler, Tom Hamer and Eric Carson. Ardwyn County School later became the Penweddig Comprehensive School.

Old College Buildings, King Street, Aberystwyth (card postmarked 1907). These buildings once formed part of a hotel (opened in 1865) which had been designed by J.P. Seddon and built by Thomas Savin of the Cambrian Railway. Following the bankruptcy of Savin, the buildings were acquired by the University in 1867 at a cost of £10,000 – about one eighth of its original cost.

Unveiling the T.C. Edwards statue, c. 1910. Thomas Charles Edwards was the first Principal of the University College at Aberystwyth, and one of those responsible for bringing the College to the town. The College admitted its first students in 1872. The ceremony is taking place outside the Old College Buildings on the sea-front.

National Library of Wales. During the nineteenth century, several fine collections of books and manuscripts were offered 'to the nation', but there was nowhere to house them. Despite extensive lobbying from Cardiff, in 1905 the Privy Council approved that a National Library should be established at Aberystwyth, and on 15 July 1911, the foundation stone was laid by Their Majesties King George V and Queen Mary.

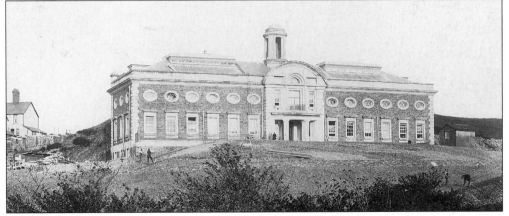

Edward Davies Laboratories (card postmarked 1907). The need for increased research facilities in the field of chemistry prompted the industrial magnate, David Davies of Llandinam, and his sisters, to donate this fine building in memory of their father. The dome in the centre later housed a wartime warning siren. When study of chemistry was discontinued c. 1990, the building was subsequently used as a department for the visual arts.

The Cadet Force attracted a substantial number of young men, and provided basic training and skills which would prove useful in later life whether the cadets chose a career in the Army or not. It is likely that National Service for young men was compulsory at the time that this photograph was taken (c. 1948). The force was led by Sergeant Major Hugh Davies.

Aberystwyth Boys' Brigade, 1909. The photograph was taken on the town's football pitch. The railway in the centreground was part of the main line from Aberystwyth to Tregaron, Lampeter

and Carmarthen. The group includes ten buglers, three side drummers and one bass drummer. Most of the boys in the photograph would now be approaching their hundredth birthday.

Aberystwyth Carnival in 1939. The Carnival is an annual event and is held in July of each year and although it was stopped for a number of years during the war, it now forms an integral part of the Aberystwyth social calendar.

The Promenade paddling pool (card postmarked in 1959). This postcard gives an indication of how busy Aberystwyth could become at the height of the season. The paddling pool was immensely popular with children. It was extensively refurbished by the Ceredigion District Council in the early 1990s. The large building in the middle distance, once the Cambria Hotel, is now the Theological College.

Seven

Monuments and Landmarks

War Memorial, Aberystwyth. This is situated at the western extremity of the Castle grounds. It was designed by an Italian architect, Dr Mario Rutelli, who arranged for the 'lady on top' to be manufactured in Italy. Following her installation and inspection, the architect suffered an attack of vertigo and had to be lowered by rope to ground level.

St Michael's church, Aberystwyth (*c.* 1915) is situated near to the waterfront, just behind the Castle Hotel, now the Old College Buildings in King Street. The extensive churchyard has been converted into a car park providing much needed funds for the church.

Gravestone outside St Michael's church, *c.* 1905. The gravestones in the churchyard have been tastefully cleared to the car park perimeter, and provide a wealth of information regarding occupations, ages, and the manner of death. That shown reads: 'My sledge & hammer lie reclined, My bellows too have lost their wind, My fire extinct, my forge decay, And in the dust my vice is laid. My coal is spent, my irons gone, My nails are drove, my work is done.'

A 367 The Gorsedd Circle, Aberystwyth

The Gorsedd Circle at Aberystwyth was placed in the Castle Grounds for use during the National Eisteddfod of Wales which was held in the town c. 1916. Each stone represents one of the Welsh counties, and has been numbered in the photograph for the convenience of the viewer: 1 – Gorsedd Stone (Maenllog); 2 – Meirioneth (Meirion); 3 – Anglesey (Mon); 4 Flint; 5 – Denbigh (Dinbych); 6 – Montgomery (Maldwyn); 7 – Radnor (Maesyfed); 8 – Monmouth (Gwent); 9 – Glamorgan (Morgannwg); 10 – Pembroke (Penfro); 11 – Carmarthen (Myrddin); 12 – Cardigan (Ceredigion); 13 – Carnarvon (Arfon); 14 – The East; 15 – Brecon.

Plâscrug Castle was built before the main Aberystwyth Castle which was built on the sea-front in 1277. Legend has it that a tunnel was dug from Plâs Crug to the Castle, a distance approaching one mile, and that gunpowder was transported through the tunnel to improve fortifications at the Castle.

The Pavilion & Pier, Aberystwyth.

Aberystwyth Pier and Pavilion (card postmarked 1914). This was a major centre for entertainment in the town. It had a long promenade on its north side leading to the pier and aviary, whereas the main Pavilion (built 1895-96) housed a cinema, entertainments and dance hall, restaurant and a conference centre.

MUNICIPAL HALL, ABERYSTWYTH. (51)

The Municipal Hall, Aberystwyth c. 1938. This was built on the site of the Waterloo Spa Hotel (which was destroyed by fire in 1919 (see p. 30). It occupied a central position in Marine Terrace and hosted many graduation ceremonies and tea dances. It later became known as King's Hall and housed an amusement arcade in its basement. It was demolished in 1989.

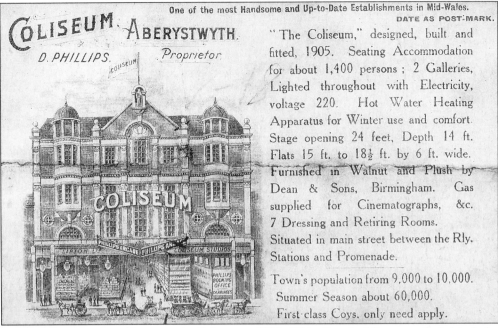

One of the most Handsome and Up-to-Date Establishments in Mid-Wales.

DATE AS POST-MARK.

COLISEUM ABERYSTWYTH.

D. PHILLIPS. Proprietor.

"The Coliseum," designed, built and fitted, 1905. Seating Accommodation for about 1,400 persons ; 2 Galleries, Lighted throughout with Electricity, voltage 220. Hot Water Heating Apparatus for Winter use and comfort. Stage opening 24 feet, Depth 14 ft. Flats 15 ft. to 18½ ft. by 6 ft. wide. Furnished in Walnut and Plush by Dean & Sons, Birmingham. Gas supplied for Cinematographs, &c. 7 Dressing and Retiring Rooms. Situated in main street between the Rly. Stations and Promenade.

Town's population from 9,000 to 10,000. Summer Season about 60,000. First-class Coys. only need apply.

Card advertising the Aberystwyth Coliseum, 1905. This fine building stands behind the Municipal Hall site, in Terrace Road. The ground floor now houses a clothes shop and information centre whereas the first floor is fully occupied by the Ceredigion Museum.

The Town Hall, Aberystwyth, c. 1910. It is recorded on the building that it dates from 1842, but it is known that the foundation stone was not laid until 1844. It was originally called the County Hall, but with the implication that it would only be used for County business, it was rechristened the Town Hall. It was seriously damaged by fire in 1957 and the opportunity was taken to restore and refurbish the building on the same site.

Statue of Queen Victoria. This wood-carved statue was once the figurehead of a ship and after it had been rescued, it was mounted on a wall in the Victoria Inn, Baker Street in 1873. To maintain the statue in pristine condition proved to be a costly exercise. It was removed from its mounting in October 1993, and is now being restored by Mr Richard Hunter.

Aberystwyth Town Clock, c. 1935. The building of this structure was commenced in 1856 at a cost of £1,250 and was presented to the town by Sir Pryse Pryse. It stood 62 feet high and housed a spiral staircase to a viewing gallery. Prior to its demolition in 1956, it was a meeting-place for many tradespeople to sell their wares.

Aberystwyth railway station in 1958. The railway station was one of the termini at the western extremity of the Cambrian Railway. It was possible to catch trains to Shrewsbury, Birmingham and London, and also to Carmarthen and Swansea. Local trains ran to Devil's Bridge and there was also a goods service to the harbour (both closed in 1931). On the first floor of the nearer block of the building, the late Margaret Evans ran an excellent permanent exhibition of old artefacts entitled 'Aberystwyth Yesterday'.

Waterloo Memorial at Pen Dinas, c. 1930. The column was commissioned in the form of a cannon by a local landowner who was present at the Battle of Waterloo. It was built by Mr W.E. Richards of Bryneithin to commemorate the victory of the Duke of Wellington. Permission to place a statue of Wellington on horseback on top of the column was withheld.

The Southgate Toll House (card postmarked in 1905). The toll-gate was built c. 1770 at the junction of the present A 487 and the A 4120 to Devil's Bridge. The house was occupied by the Collector of the Turnpike Tolls, and, in 1871, his name was Thomas Lewis. In 1959, the entire building was transferred to the Welsh Folk Museum at St Fagans near Cardiff where it was re-erected.

Caradoc Road, Aberystwyth, c. 1912. This card shows one of the streets adjoining Llanbadarn Road, and the architecture employed for a great many of the residences in Aberystwyth. It was one of the main thoroughfares to the former Aberystwyth Infirmary, and now leads to the Bronglais General Hospital.

The Cliff Railway, Aberystwyth (card postmarked in 1906), only ten years after it was built by the Aberystwyth Improvement Company. It originally operated on the water-balance principle but this was discontinued in 1922 when the railway became electrically powered. It is arguably the longest cable-hauled railway in Europe.

The staff of the Cliff Railway, *c*. 1910.

Statue of Thomas Edward Ellis. In 1872, the University College took in its first 'batch' of twenty-six students. It was only three years after this that Ellis was admitted. Within twenty years, student numbers had increased to 200, and in 1892 T.E. Ellis became the first president of the Old Students' Association. Having served as a Member of Parliament for a number of years, he died in his early forties.

Eight
Sporting Activities

Aberystwyth Town football team, 1907-08. The collection in this book alone indicates that all in all, the town of Aberystwyth has a large number of football teams. The ultimate ambition of most players in these teams was to play for the Aberystwyth Town team in front of their home crowd at Park Avenue.

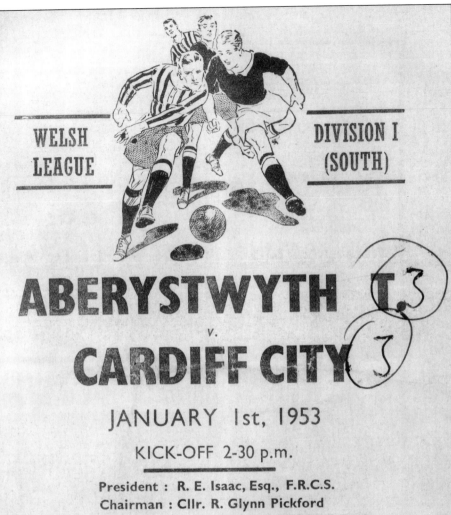

WELSH LEAGUE

DIVISION I (SOUTH)

ABERYSTWYTH

v.

CARDIFF CITY

JANUARY 1st, 1953

KICK-OFF 2-30 p.m.

President : R. E. Isaac, Esq., F.R.C.S.
Chairman : Cllr. R. Glynn Pickford
Treasurer : Mr. H. Emrys Jones, Midland Bank
Secretary : Cllr. W. G. Hopkins,
Marina Vista, Cliff Terrace
Team Manager : Mr. Bryn Davies

HEADQUARTERS : TALBOT HOTEL   Tel. 575

A.F.C. Official Programme 2d

Printed and Published by the Cambrian News (Aberystwyth) Ltd

Official programme for the match between Aberystwyth Town and Cardiff City in 1953. Although every 'small' football team has its moment of glory, on this occasion, the town were playing the City reserves. The visiting team were aspiring professional football players – indeed many had already signed the necessary papers. The result on this occasion was a very creditable 3-3 draw.

Aberystwyth YMCA football team, *c.* 1950. Some communities within the town, such as Penparcau, fielded more than one football team. The team fielded by the YMCA was always at or near the top of the Aberystwyth & District Football League.

Penparcau Rovers football team, 1909-10 season. The community of Penparcau has always been a stronghold of football in the town and until recently would only release their 'play-ground' for road development purposes on condition that a suitable alternative could be found.

Trefechan football team, *c.* 1932. Trefechan is a small community between Penparcau and the town centre. The group is known to include Messrs Edwards (builder – Dinas Terrace), Davies, Loveday, John Edwards, Bertie Bradley, Billy Isaac (goalkeeper), Bert Morgan, Daniels (garage services).

Dinas (School) football team during the 1949-50 season in the charge of Headmaster Watkins and Physical Training Teacher Mr Gravell. Schools played a very competitive part in the promotion of soccer within the town.

The above photograph shows the Aber Gas Works Football Team *c.* 1950. Many employers and organisations within the town formed their own sports teams. The goalkeeper at this time was Mr Goronwy ('Groxy') Edwards who became chief maintenance engineer on the Colleges' campus at Llanbadarn, and also a much respected local councillor.

Cardiganshire Police football team, 1933-34 season. The headquarters of the Cardiganshire Police was at Aberystwyth, and the force was, of course, large enough to form its own football team.

Great Western Railway football team, 1923-24 season. Aberystwyth became an important railway terminus and in common with many other organisations in the town, the Great Western Railway sported its own football team which became known as the Locos.

The ladies were not to be left behind. The Eirwen Cleaning Company provided a laundry and dry cleaning service in the town, and their team comprised of, from left to right, front row: Ruth James, Margaret Wilson, Megan Mason, Ethell Bell (captain), Freda Evans, Joan Toy, and Gwladys Massey. Back row: Mr Albert Davies (referee) Gwen Jones, Noreen Dawson, Nancy Putt, Gwladys Rufus, Mr George Lewis (trainer).

In 1922, the Tan-y-Cae Junior football team were a very successful club. In that year, they won the prestigious Albert Davies Cup. The above photograph shows them displaying their cup and medals. The trophies had been presented by Mr Albert Davies – a local fishmonger who was always supportive of football activity in the town. The medals were handsome mementoes, made of solid silver as the hallmark on the reverse side proved.

1922
TANYCAU F C
WINNERS
ALBERT DAVIES
FOOTBALL TROPHY

The Aberystwyth Youth rugby team in 1962. The group is known to include Roy Jones, Mansel Williams, Michael ?, Chris Edwards, David Lewis, David Price, Michael Nicholls, Brian Davies, Geraint Jenkins and Gwyn ?.

Aberystwyth Bowling Greens (card postmarked 1942). Although the town has two open-air bowling greens, the one shown here is that adjacent to Plâscrug Avenue. The green itself appears to be in good shape, but the facility is relatively undeveloped.

Plascrug Bowling Green, *c.* 1952. The immediate post-war years saw significant improvements in the facilities with the addition of its pavilion, built in the left foreground (above). These two cards testify to the popularity of the sport in the town. In the background (below) can be seen the Edward Davies Laboratories (see page 83).

Men's Rowing Club at the University College of Wales (Aberystwyth), 1925-26. Rowing was popular with students of both sexes at the University for nearly eighty years but interest waned completely in the early 1960s. It is interesting to note that the town now has at least two ladies' longboat rowing teams.

Ladies' rowing team at the University College of Wales (Aberystwyth), c. 1923. The team comprised of Mona G. Williams, E. Lloyd Jones, Hilda Thompson, Dorothy M. Roberts, Mabel K. Evans, E.J. Fry, Gladys Cooper, Doreen Smith and Annie Harris. Their coach was 'Jack the Boatman'; in a contemporary newspaper article, the Aberystwyth columnist, Will O'Whispers conceded that 'I have not been able to find out Jack the Boatman's surname or where he lives'.

108

Cardiganshire Police cricket team, *c.* 1950. The photograph was taken on the Vicarage playing fields at Llanbadarn Road. Chief Constable Jones presides over the team which is known to include Inspector Ken Williams, Sergeant Thomas, and Police Constables Jenkins and Hywel Williams.

THE NEW TENNIS COURTS, EN TOUT CAS, ABERYSTWYTH.

Aberystwyth Tennis Courts, *c.* 1934. The tennis courts occupy part of the space between North Road and Queen's Road. The 'en tout cas' is taken to refer to the all-weather nature of the court surfaces, and this in turn led to great popularity and heavy demand.

University College of Wales (Aberystwyth) Harriers, 1920-21, with, from left to right, back row: Mellish, Morley, Bassett, W.R. Jones, H. Jones and J.H. Evans. Front row: Williams, Llewellyn, Thomas, Dai Lewis (captain), T.J. Thomas, Wallis and W. Evans.

Nine
Celebrities and Characters

'Last of the Summer Wine' was the name that was affectionately given to this photograph. Mr Cyril Blackwell (left) was, at one time, an undertaker, but later carried out a great deal of carpentry and interior decorating work at the hospital. Mr Willie Andy (centre) was a forester with a very keen interest in photography. Along with Mrs Mary Pugh, the three became firm friends. Ralph Kenyon photographed them at the top of Great Darkgate Street on a public seat which they (along with local townsfolk) came to regard as their own.

The visit of Amy Johnson to Aberystwyth. Miss Johnson and her husband Jim Mollison came to Aberystwyth to seek sponsorship for Amy's forthcoming solo flight to Australia. She and her husband are photographed on the steps of the Queen's Hotel at the end of Marine Terrace – buildings which have since been converted to County Offices (see page 47).

Sir John J. Gibson of the *Cambrian News*. Although the *Cambrian News* started its life in the English border town of Oswestry, in 1873, John Gibson was given the responsibility of organising and editing the paper at Aberystwyth, a job which was to last for forty years. He led a controversial existence often being 'condemned' for articles for which he was not responsible. In 1915, he was knighted for his services to journalism.

Aberystwyth celebrities by Matt of the *Sunday Graphic*, c. 1932.

BRITISH TRANSPORT COMMISSION

Permit Bearer *Mr. G. Morgan, wife & 3 children.*

to No. 3 Platform

ABERYSTWYTH STATION

on

Monday, August 8th, 1955

to witness the arrival of

HER MAJESTY QUEEN ELIZABETH II.

AND

HIS ROYAL HIGHNESS THE DUKE OF EDINBURGH

Admittance by this invitation only and NOT after 9.0 a.m.

Signed .... Station Master

Invitation for the Royal visit, 1955. Aberystwyth was graced with another Royal visit in 1955. The Queen was to arrive by train, and the invitation above was one of the 'perks' which were given to railway staff and their families.

Nineteenth-century Aberystwyth traders' carts. The late Mrs Margaret Evans MBE was responsible for assembling a magnificent collection of memorabilia and artefacts which were displayed in a permanent exhibition entitled 'Aberystwyth Yesterday'. This recent photograph shows part of her collection of traders' carts, at the top of Great Darkgate Street.

Opposite: The Royal visit to Aberystwyth in 1955. HM Queen Elizabeth II accompanied by the Duke of Edinburgh visited the town in 1955 to open the extension to the National Library of Wales. She was escorted from the Royal Train by Mr George Rowlands, a school teacher from Ardwyn Grammar School.

Auctioneer's staff, *c.* 1950. Mr Richard ('Dick') Morgan was a highly successful auctioneer, valuer and estate agent in the immediate post-war years. He is posed here with his (aproned) staff, Mr I. Hawkins, Mr Albert Wilson and Mr David James (extreme right), outside the sales room in St James Square where he regularly conducted furniture sales.

Roots of the Revivalist Movement (card postmarked 1905). The Revd T.Evan Roberts was Minister of Siloh Chapel from 1895 onwards, and from 1904 to 1906 there was considerable interest throughout Wales in his evangelical sermons. Siloh was one of the leading Methodist chapels in Wales. He retired in 1925. Both his son and grandson were solicitors in the firm of Humphrey Roberts & Bott.

Soft drinks manufacture at Aberystwyth, *c.* 1953. The firm of Thomas & Evans established their highly successful Corona Soft Drinks Company at Porth in the Rhondda. It was not long before they established a factory at Trefechan in Aberystwyth. The picture shows two of their delivery men – Messrs Peter Bland and Evan Edwards.

Staff of the Corona depot at Trefechan pose for the photograph *c.* 1953.

Captain Thomas Williams, coxswain of the Aberystwyth lifeboat.

An Aberystwyth fisherman, *c.* 1895.

Ten
Aberystwyth at War and Sea

Tank on the Promenade, *c.* 1917. This particular vehicle visited Aberystwyth in the latter part of the First World War during 'War Weapons Week', a project mounted to raise money for the war effort. This vehicle should not be confused with the tank which was originally sited in North Parade but later moved to the sea-front between the Waterloo and Belle Vue hotels and which remained there for some twenty years, but was finally removed and used for munitions purposes at the outbreak of the Second World War.

Soldiers in training at Aberystwyth, *c.* 1914. This was a proud moment for young Harold Edwards of Tanycastell, South Road as he posed with soldiers who were billeted at his home while undertaking their training at Aberystwyth.

Soldiers in training at Aberystwyth. From 1914 onwards, new recruits were sent to the town for their basic training. These South Wales Borderers were billeted at Stafford House on the Promenade.

Soldiers in training at Aberystwyth (card postmarked 1915). Basic training included bayonet practice; this involved soldiers running and 'stabbing' one of the straw-filled sacks hanging in the background while, at the same time, making as much intimidatory noise as possible.

Soldiers in convalescence at Aberystwyth (card postmarked 1916). The Theological College on the sea-front became a hospital for convalescing soldiers from November 1915 until the end of First World War hostilities. Patients wore a grey uniform and red neckerchief.

The Territorials at Aberystwyth, *c*. 1912. The Territorial Army held a camp each summer in the years before the First World War which was mainly concerned with route marches and the occasional mock battle. Surprisingly, many recruits regarded a fortnight at camp as their annual holiday.

The Territorials at Aberystwyth, *c*. 1912. Naturally, all the 'Terriers' needed adequate feeding at the start and end of each day. This responsibility fell to men such as those shown above.

The Cardiganshire Home Guard. Men who may have been a little too old for front-line service during the Second World War often volunteered to undertake service in the Home Guard. The men were divided into a number of different sections, each section having a different function to fulfil. Above is shown the Signals Section of the 1st Battalion. Their headquarters were in the barracks in Park Avenue. They also made use of a firing-range at Tanybwlch.

The Cardiganshire Home Guard, showing the senior officers of 'B' Company of the 1st Cardiganshire Home Guard. Back row: Sgt. E.T. Griffiths, CSM D.J. Evans, CQMS R.T. Jones, Sergeants J. Oliver, T. Price, W.T. Benbow and Edwin Jones. Middle row: Lieutenants D.W. Jones, Seth Williams, Gwyn Jones, G.A. Evans, E.J. George and W.G. Pryse. Front row: Lieutenants T.O. Thomas, R.S. Thomas, Capt. D.J. Roberts, Major W.J. Rowlands, Lieutenants D.J. Williams, J.R.W. Jenkins and E.D. Bailey.

The Children's paddling pool (pictured in July 1911) existed at the extreme western end of the Promenade and could be used by children at low tide. The Royal Naval vessels visited Aberystwyth at the same time as King George V and Queen Mary came to the town for the purpose of laying the foundation stone for the National Library of Wales.

HMS *Furious* off Aberystwyth.

The harbour at Aberystwyth (card postmarked July 1905). Like many Welsh ports, the use of Aberystwyth as a trading port was severely restricted by the bar at the mouth of the Ystwyth and Rheidol rivers. When the bar was dredged and the substantial stone pier built in the late 1830s, this enabled ships up to 650 tons to use the port. Increased commercial activity on the railway, however, reduced the importance of seaborne trade from Aberystwyth and by 1925, trading at the port was in steep decline.

Yachts in Bay, Aberystwyth

Fishing in Cardigan Bay (card postmarked 1924). The photograph shows the 'nobby boats' off the beach at Aberystwyth. The 'nobbies' were a fleet of fishing boats from Morecambe in Lancashire which made regular trips to Cardigan Bay presumably drift netting for the apparently limitless supply of herring.

Fishermen on the beach, *c.* 1935. There were (and still are) many boat-owners who offered fishing trips, particularly at the height of the holiday season. Here, a number of holiday-makers, along with the 'professionals', proudly display their catch of mackerel on the beach. The bandstand and pleasure-rowing-boats are worthy of note.

SAILING BOATS ON BEACH. ABERYSTWYTH.

Aberystwyth pleasure-boats (postmarked 1928) – these included such craft as the *Pride of the Midlands*, *Mauretania*, *Birmingham City* and *Worcester Castle*, all of which would vie for trade in offering 'trips round the bay'. Some, of course, ventured further afield, and when weather permitted, Aberdovey was a popular destination.

The *Mauretania* (card postmarked 1912) was a similar vessel, named no doubt after the liner which was, at the time, the largest and fastest vessel afloat. She was owned by Mr David Williams who was coxswain of the Aberystwyth lifeboat and Harry Davies, a member of the Royal Naval Reserve.

Aberystwyth harbour, c. 1895, in a somewhat unkempt state. It does, however, show the size of some of the vessels which were using the port at this time. Those in the foreground are probably awaiting repair. The railway line in the foreground was an extension of the narrow-gauge Vale of Rheidol railway which was extensively used to carry slate and mineral ores to the port. Tanybwlch beach lies between the harbour and the mountain beyond.

Acknowledgements

In preparing this book, very little assistance has been sought from sources external to the Aberystwyth Postcard Club (APC). The club, however, would like to record its grateful thanks to (a) Mr Michael Freeman for writing a very thoughtful foreword to this volume, and (b) Mr Simon Eckley of the Chalford Publishing Company, for his constant support to the Club, despite one life threatening trip to the town in the depths of a winter snow storm. As Club Chairman, however, I am deeply grateful to twelve of our members who gave up many evenings during the year, giving of their expertise and providing material. In this connection, I would like to record my warmest thanks to Mrs Audrey Baron-Jones, Mr Ron Cowell, Mrs Doreen Davies, Mr Jack Day, Mrs Olga Edwards, Mr Peter Henley, The Reverend Ronnie Hughes, Mrs Wendy Phillips, Mrs William Troughton, Mrs Anne Wilson and Mr Bob Yates. All have given freely of their time and effort, and supported the venture at times when it would have been easiest to abandon the whole project.

Over the past ten months, the APC have had great enjoyment in compiling this book, and sincerely hope that everyone who reads it will share this pleasure. None of us were prepared for the long hours of work involved, and would like to take this opportunity of thanking our Chairman, Mr Martin Lewis who guided us along each step of the way, undertook a 100 mile round trip each time the Club met, liaised with the Publishers and co-ordinated the entire effort. Without his invaluable assistance, it is likely that readers would not now be enjoying this insight into the recent history of Aberystwyth.